COYOTES AND WOLVES CHARGE!

WILD PETS GONE WRONG

Gareth Stevens PUBLISHING

DERRICK RICHARDS

Please visit our website, www.garethstevens.com. For a free color catalog of all our high-quality books, call toll free 1-800-542-2595 or fax 1-877-542-2596

Cataloging-in-Publication Data
Names: Richard, Derrick.
Title: Coyotes and wolves charge! / Derrick Richards.
Description: Buffalo, NY : Gareth Stevens Publishing, 2027. | Series: Wild pets gone wrong | Includes glossary and index.
Identifiers: ISBN 9781482479751 (pbk.) | ISBN 9781482479768 (library bound) | ISBN 9781482479775 (ebook)
Subjects: LCSH: Coyote–Juvenile literature. | Wolves–Juvenile literature. | Wild animals as pets–Juvenile literature.
Classification: LCC QL737.C22 R534 2027 | DDC 599.7725–dc23

Portions of this work were originally authored by Barbara Linde and published as When Pets Attack!: Coyotes and Wolves are Not Pets! All new material in this edition is authored by Derrick Richards.

Published in 2027 by
Gareth Stevens Publishing
2544 Clinton Street
Buffalo, NY 14224

Designer: Beeline Media and Design
Editor: Tricia Hoffman

Photo credits: Cover, p. 1 Holly S Cannon/Shutterstock.com; cover, p. 1 queezz (background texture)/Shutterstock.com; cover, p. 1, 4, 7, 9, 11, 12, 15, 16, 19, 20, 23, 24, 27, 29 Tartila (sidebar background)/Shutterstock.com; p. 3, 4, 7, 8, 12, 15, 16, 20, 23, 24, 27, 30, 31, 32 Nadia Chi (background texture)/Shutterstock.com; p. 5 Mircea Costina/Shutterstock.com; p. 6 Kjetil Kolbjornsrud/Shutterstock.com; p. 6 Annette Shaff/Shutterstock.com; p. 8 Warren Metcalf/Shutterstock.com; p. 8 Unfiltered Adventures/Shutterstock.com; p. 10 Holly Kuchera/Shutterstock.com; p. 12 Teguh Mujiono/Shutterstock.com; p. 13 Michael Roeder/Shutterstock.com; p. 14 Matt Knoth/Shutterstock.com; p. 16 NPS/Neal Herbert/NPS; p. 17 NPS Photo/Kent Miller/NPS; p. 18 outdoorsman/Shutterstock.com; p. 21 Vagengeim/Shutterstock.com; p. 25 Doug Oglesby/Shutterstock.com; p. 26 Thyrymn2/Shutterstock.com; p. 28 Matt Knoth/Shutterstock.com; p. 29 TMP - An Instant of Time/Shutterstock.com; p. 22, 23 Tatiana Murr/Shutterstock.com

Printed in China

CPSIA compliance information: Batch #QS27GS: For further information contact Gareth Stevens, New York, New York at 1-800-542-2595.

CONTENTS

Meet the Canines

Coyotes, wolves, and dogs are all canines. About 15,000 years ago, some wolves became **domesticated**. Scientists think hungry wolves stayed near human settlements, eating scraps. Over time, these wolves became tame. People figured out how to train the wolves as helpers. The dogs we love as pets are the **descendants** of these animals.

Coyotes are related to both dogs and wolves. However, no matter how much your dog looks like a wolf or a coyote, only the dog is a pet. Wolves and coyotes are wild animals! They do not make good pets.

THE FIRST DOGS

Scientists study the bones of ancient wolves and dogs. That's how they're able to figure out how and when dogs probably first became domesticated. Dogs you see today haven't been around for long, though. The oldest dog breeds are no more than 500 years old, and most date only from about 150 years ago!

This is a coyote, but coyotes and wolves look alike. It is sometimes hard to tell the difference between them.

Gray wolves can weigh up to 150 pounds (68 kg), but coyotes are smaller. They usually weigh 50 pounds (23 kg) or less.

Let's Compare

Dogs come in all shapes and sizes. Teacup Yorkshire terriers can weigh as little as 2 pounds (0.9 kg). Huge Great Danes can weigh up to 175 pounds (79 kg). Coyotes and wolves are somewhere in between. Wolves are larger than coyotes.

Coyotes and wolves are both **omnivores**. They chow down on just about anything from fruits and vegetables to grass and flowers. They eat small animals, such as birds, snakes, and mice. But they also hunt large animals, such as elk, deer, and moose. They eat a lot at one time if they can. They may go days before eating again.

CHECK THE FOOTPRINTS

Looking at tracks can help you identify an animal as a wolf or coyote. Wolf tracks are farther apart than coyote tracks.

Life in the Pack

Wolves and coyotes are both social animals. They live in packs. They form male and female pairs when it's time to mate. These pairs often stay together for life. The animals build a dry, cozy den in a cave, under the ground, in a log, or in another sheltered spot. A female coyote may have as many as six pups at a time. A female wolf has as many as 11 pups.

Wolves and coyotes live up to 14 years in the wild. They may live much longer in zoos and other protected areas.

The whole pack takes care of the pups. The pups drink their mothers' milk until they're old enough to eat food. Then, they will learn to hunt from other adults in the pack.

SPEAK UP!

Coyotes and wolves howl for many reasons. They howl to greet other members of the pack. They howl to call the pack together to hunt. They howl extra loud to warn other animals to stay away. If you think your dog makes a lot of noise, that's nothing compared to a coyote or wolf!

Scientists believe that coyotes first arrived on the East Coast of the United States in the early 1900s.

Where Do Coyotes Live?

In the 1700s, the coyote lived in western North America. One of its main predators was the wolf. As people began settling these areas, they killed many wolves. As a result, the number of coyotes increased, and they took over wolf **habitats**.

When these areas got crowded, coyotes moved eastward. The wolves in the east had already died out. Coyotes easily **adapt** to new surroundings, so the move was successful. Now, their **range** includes most of the United States, from West Coast to East Coast. They also live throughout most of Canada and Mexico.

COYOTE STORIES

Coyotes were important to Indigenous American people. They appear often in American Indian tales. Coyotes are tricksters who try to fool people or other animals. They're often outwitted, however. In some tales, the coyote is the creature that made the first people.

Where Do Wolves Live?

It's thought that at one time, there were almost two million wolves on Earth. They used to live across most of North America, Europe, and Asia. However, wolves have been harmed by habitat loss and humans. People have long feared wolves, because they're so fierce. Over time, people hunted them until they became **endangered** and nearly **extinct**. Laws had to be made to protect them.

Now, there are fewer than 250,000 wolves worldwide. Many of them live in Alaska, Canada, or Asia.

WOLF STORIES

Wolves are often the evil characters in fairy tales. Think about "The Three Little Pigs" or "Little Red Riding Hood." However, wolves are heroes in other stories. In Roman myths, a wolf raised two boys named Romulus and Remus. They were the children of the god Mars, and they later founded the city of Rome.

Wolves need a lot of open space to hunt. Wolf packs will claim territories just for them.

Coyotes are ***scavengers****. They will eat whatever they can find.*

Coyotes are Valuable

Coyotes are important to their habitats. Coyotes are even useful to people in cities and towns. They eat rats, bugs, and birds, so they help control these populations. Farmers and gardeners are often happy to have coyotes dine on weasels, moles, and other pests. When coyotes have eaten their fill, smaller animals move in and eat the leftovers.

Coyotes also eat old and **diseased** animals. Removing these animals helps the rest of the population and the whole habitat. Without coyotes, some animal populations might grow too large. This could lead to more and more problems.

LAWS FOR PROTECTION

The Endangered Species Act (ESA) once provided **federal** protections for wolves. These laws helped their populations grow. There are no federal laws protecting coyotes. They are not an endangered species.

Wolves are Valuable Too

Long ago, wolves roamed freely in Yellowstone National Park in Wyoming. As more people visited and hunted in the park, the wolves were killed off. Because wolves eat elk and coyotes, the populations of those animals got larger. But unfortunately, there wasn't enough food for them, and many starved. The elk also damaged numerous trees and plants.

Wolves were put back into Yellowstone in 1995. Elk and coyote numbers went down. Other animals and birds eat wolves' leftovers, so there was more food for them too. The populations thrived.

WOLF-WATCHING

Visitors to Yellowstone can drive or walk through parts of the park to see wolves. There are rules about how far away visitors should stay. Winter is the easiest time of year to see wolves in the park, because you can more easily spot their coats against the snow.

About 500 wolves now live in Yellowstone National Park. Some of the wolves wear radio collars so wildlife experts can keep track of them.

Even wolves and coyotes that were raised by people their whole lives keep their wild instincts.

Caring for Canines

No matter how cute and cuddly coyote and wolf pups are, they're still wild animals. Some people raise pups as pets. This isn't a good idea. When pups grow to be adults, their **instincts** take over. They fight to become the **dominant** member of the pack—and they may fight you!

Wild canines are hard to train. You can never be sure if they'll obey you. Many groups are against owning wild animals as pets. They think it's dangerous for people to try to control the animals. It's also unhealthy—and even cruel—for the animals.

MARKING THEIR TERRITORY

Wolves and coyotes mark the areas where they live. They do this by leaving their waste to warn off other animals. You don't want them doing this in your house!

Not Pets!

Coyotes and wolves are used to living in packs, not alone or with people. They're also outdoor animals. They won't want to stay in your house. Even if you have a huge backyard, they'll feel cramped. And they may even try to attack other pets—or even people!

Your hungry pet needs to eat, and remember that coyotes and wolves eat meat. Where will you get all the fresh food your wild pet wants?

Just like regular pets, coyotes and wolves may get sick or carry diseases. Unlike your dog or cat, however, many veterinarians won't treat wild animals. In some states, it's against the law for them to do so!

A HELPING HAND

If you really want to be around wild animals, **volunteer** at a local wildlife park or shelter. Many of these places raise injured wild animals or those that have been dropped off by people who can't take care of them anymore. You can be helpful to those poor animals and learn a lot about them too.

Huskies, Alaskan malamutes, and German shepherds are dogs that look and act like wolves, because they are closely related. These animals make much better pets!

If you see a wolf or coyote in the wild, do not feed it! Feeding wild coyotes and wolves only encourages them to get closer to people, which can result in attacks.

Wolf Attacks

Wolves in the wild usually avoid people. But it's difficult to avoid them if people come into their territories. Since 2002, more than 25 people have died from wolf attacks throughout the world. One of those was in the United States.

In June 2012, a zoo worker in Sweden was attacked and killed by wolves. She had entered a cage with eight wolves alone, as she had done since they were pups. No one is exactly sure what happened.

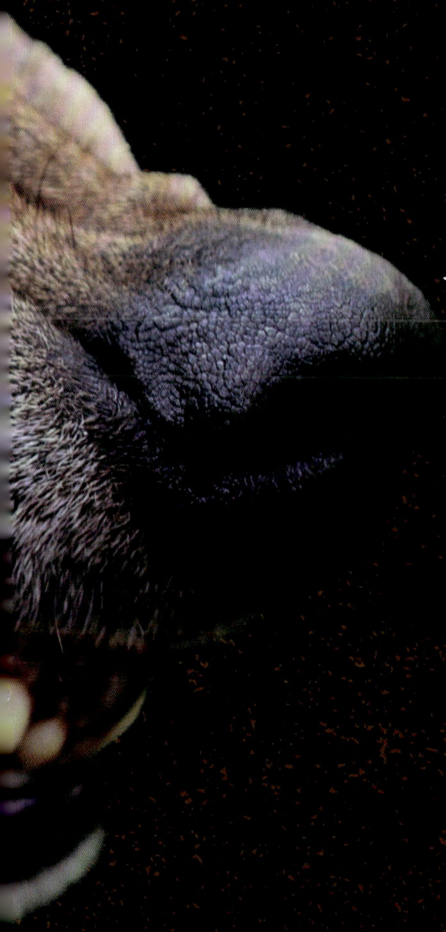

A DEADLY DISEASE

Rabies is a disease that can kill animals and people. A person can get rabies if bitten or scratched by an animal that has rabies. If the person gets medicine in time and if the injuries aren't too severe, the person will recover. Some people who work around animals get rabies shots to prevent the disease.

Coyote Attacks

Coyotes have attacked at least 160 people in the United States in the past 40 years. Two people have died from coyote attacks—a 3-year-old girl who was attacked in her driveway and a 19-year-old female hiker.

In 2006, a coyote that had rabies tried to get into a house in Pennsylvania. The homeowners' two dogs battled the coyote until the homeowners killed it.

In December 2012, three coyotes attacked a man and his dog in his backyard in Washington State. The man was scratched and bitten before he finally shook off the coyotes. He got several rabies shots afterward, but luckily survived the attack.

ALL ABOARD!

In February 2002, a coyote walked through an open train door at the Portland International Airport—and took a seat! Luckily, no riders were on the train. An airport wildlife specialist captured the animal. He moved it to a wilderness area beyond the airport.

Coyotes seem to attack young, small children the most. Attacks on adult humans are less common.

*Attacks have been increasing in recent years, especially in **urban** areas.*

Protect Yourself

You're not likely to be attacked by a coyote or wolf. But it's still best to know how to protect yourself, just in case.

First, never walk alone in a wild area. A group of people is **intimidating** to wild animals. If you're alone and see a coyote or wolf, don't run. Stand your ground. Then, yell, wave your arms, and try to look scary. You can even throw sticks and rocks. If they still approach, try punching them on the nose. If all else fails, climb the nearest tree and call for help.

DON'T RUN

Never run away from an attacking coyote or wolf. Coyotes and wolves are more likely to attack someone if they're running away. This is what their other prey does. Remember, these predators are expert hunters. They'll chase you, and they're much faster than the fastest person.

Living in Peace

In Denver, Colorado, park staff came up with a plan for coyotes and people to coexist, or live peacefully in the same areas. It's called hazing.

Coyotes had been seen frequently at the park when people were walking their dogs. People were scared. So trained wildlife workers went to the park every morning at the same time. They banged pots, blew whistles, and made a lot of noise. After a few weeks, the coyotes stopped coming to the park in the morning. The workers trained the local people in their hazing methods.

This plan worked well. But remember—coexistence is not the same thing as having a wild animal as a pet. That is never a wise choice!

Wild animals should be respected when you're in their space.

COEXISTING

There have been recent coyote sightings in large cities like Los Angeles, Chicago, and New York City. With the amount of food available in these places, coyotes may be people's neighbors for a long time.

Glossary

adapt: to change to suit new conditions

descendant: an animal that comes from an animal of an earlier time

diseased: having an illness

domesticate: to raise an animal so it can live with or be used by people

dominant: the most powerful or strongest

endangered: in danger of dying out

extinct: no longer living

federal: relating to the national government

habitat: the natural place where an animal or plant lives

instinct: an inborn reaction or behavior that aids in survival

intimidate: to create a feeling of fear or awe in a person or animal

omnivore: an animal that eats both plants and animals

range: the area where something lives

scavenger: animals that eat meat left by other animals

urban: having to do with living in a big city

volunteer: a person who works without being paid

More Information

Books

Bolte, Mari. *Coyotes.* The Creative Company, 2025.

Schwartz, Heather E. *Dogs and Wolves.* Pebble, 2025.

Websites

Coyote
www.nationalgeographic.com/animals/mammals/facts/coyote
Watch a video about coyotes and hear what they sound like.

Gray Wolf
www.nationalgeographic.com/animals/mammals/facts/gray-wolf
Learn more about gray wolves at National Geographic.

In the Valley of the Wolves
www.pbs.org/wnet/nature/episodes/in-the-valley-of-the-wolves/video-full-episode/4678/
This PBS video tells the story of a Yellowstone wolf pack.

Publisher's note to educators and parents: *Our editors have carefully reviewed these websites to ensure that they are suitable for students. Many websites change frequently, however, and we cannot guarantee that a site's future contents will continue to meet our high standards of quality and educational value. Be advised that students should be closely supervised whenever they access the Internet.*

Index